Intervention to Stop
and Mass Atrocities
International Norms and U.S. Policy

COUNCIL on FOREIGN RELATIONS

International Institutions and Global Governance Program

Council Special Report No. 49
October 2009

Matthew C. Waxman

Intervention to Stop Genocide and Mass Atrocities

International Norms and U.S. Policy

Mixed Sources
Product group from well-managed forests and other controlled sources
www.fsc.org   Cert no. SW-COC-001530
© 1996 Forest Stewardship Council

Contents

Foreword

On a stone wall at the memorial of the Dachau concentration camp, a promise is written in five languages: "Never Again." Yet in the decades since the Holocaust, in places from Cambodia to Rwanda to Darfur, international actors have failed to mount an effective response to mass atrocities.

The reasons for this failure are numerous. Political will to act, as well as the availability and capability of military intervention forces, is often absent. Moreover, enduring notions of sovereignty make it difficult for outside countries or international organizations to step in, despite considerable acceptance in recent years of the concept of "responsibility to protect."

Another important part of this debate concerns the international legal system governing the use of force in situations of actual or potential atrocities. In this Council Special Report, Matthew C. Waxman asks whether this legal regime is effective in preventing and stopping such crimes. The report notes that international legal practices constrain swift action and require extensive consultation, especially in the United Nations Security Council, before particular steps can be taken. Waxman, though, argues that the system has certain benefits: it can confer legitimacy and help actors coordinate both military and non-military efforts to prevent or stop atrocities. He also contends that different arrangements of the kind some have proposed would be unlikely to prove more effective.

He therefore opposes wholesale reforms but recommends more modest steps the United States could take to improve the current legal regime. These measures include expressing strong but nuanced support for the responsibility to protect and working with other permanent members of the UN Security Council to discourage the use of vetoes in clear cases of mass atrocities. But the report also argues that the United States must be prepared to act alone or with others in urgent cases without Security Council approval.

With thorough analysis and thoughtful recommendations, Waxman points the way toward an international legal system capable of promoting timely and effective action in cases of mass atrocities. This is a topic central to ongoing debates about the limits of sovereignty and the responsibility of states for their own citizens and others. It is also a subject that must be addressed if "Never Again" is to become a reality rather than a slogan.

Richard N. Haass
President
Council on Foreign Relations
October 2009

Acknowledgments

I am grateful to this report's advisory committee members for generously lending their expert insight, suggestions, and support. I am also grateful to CFR President Richard N. Haass and Director of Studies James M. Lindsay, as well as to CFR colleagues Micah Zenko and Paul B. Stares for their guidance during the project. Several other outside experts provided valuable comments along the way, including Todd Buchwald, William Burke-White, Michael Doyle, and Michael Mattler. Several CFR staff members have significantly contributed to this project: Assistant Director of Studies Melanie Gervacio Lin, my research associate Gideon Copple, and Patricia Dorff and Lia Norton in Publications.

The Jolie-Pitt Foundation sponsored this research effort, and I am very grateful for its generosity. I also thank CFR Vice President for Communications and Marketing Lisa Shields for her valuable advice and help as liaison. This report was crafted under the auspices of CFR's International Institutions and Global Governance program, led by Stewart M. Patrick, who deserves particular thanks for his superb guidance.

Although many have contributed to this endeavor from conception to publication, the findings and recommendations herein are my own, and I accept full responsibility for them.

Matthew C. Waxman

Council Special Report

Introduction

The collective international failure to stop genocidal violence and resulting humanitarian catastrophe in Sudan prompts the familiar question of whether the United States or, more broadly, the international community has the political will and capabilities necessary to deter or stop mass atrocities. It is well understood that mobilizing domestic and international political support as well as leveraging diplomatic, economic, and maybe even military tools are necessary to stop mass atrocities, though they may not always be enough. Other studies have focused, therefore, on what steps the United States and its international partners could take to build capabilities of the sort needed to prevent, stop, and remedy these crimes. This report approaches the problem from a different angle and asks whether the current international legal regime with regard to the use of military force—that is, international law regulating the resort to armed intervention—is appropriate and effective in deterring and stopping mass atrocities.

This report concludes that the current international legal regime *could* be effective in stopping mass atrocities and that none of the often-proposed radical reforms to international law will be more effective in the short term. To best combat the threat of mass atrocities consistent with other U.S. foreign policy interests and priorities, the United States should take independent steps and work with allies to improve the responsiveness of the existing UN Security Council system while preparing and signaling a willingness, if the UN Security Council fails to act in future mass atrocity crises, to take necessary action to address them. The major elements of a strategy should include strong but nuanced declarations of support for the "responsibility to protect," a diplomatic effort to work with like-minded allies on common commitments to the responsibility to protect and redoubled engagement with other states to explain the U.S. position, and integration of this outreach with U.S. diplomacy on other international legal issues.

The report's objectives are simultaneously ambitious and modest. They are ambitious in that they aim ultimately to address a problem that has confounded policymakers and pits traditional notions of state sovereignty and concern for protecting human rights against each other. The objectives are modest, however, insofar as this report reflects no pretense that these crises can all be solved militarily, or by reforming international law, or principally by the United States and its allies. In emphasizing international norms related to intervention in mass atrocity crises, this report does not intend to emphasize the primacy of military means or coercive approaches; rather, it aims to improve the use of intervention in a supporting role and when other means are likely to be ineffective.[1]

Besides its specific recommendations, a broader goal of this report is to integrate the study of strategy and law or norms—in other words, collective expectation for the proper behavior of states.[2] Too often, the policy community and the international law community speak past each other on these issues: policy studies focus on political will and capabilities, relegating legal issues to a distant secondary concern; legal analyses focus on legal principles and precedents without adequate attention to their impact on policy effectiveness. This report brings together the study of strategy and law by emphasizing how political will and capabilities are not independent of international law but are shaped by it, and how the normative terrain of intervention can affect operations on the ground.

Deterring and Stopping Mass Atrocities: Policy Challenges

Several major policy studies during the past decade have examined how the United States and its international partners can better meet the challenges of preventing and stopping mass atrocities, including genocide and systematic ethnic cleansing. It seems that every major crisis of this sort, such as Rwanda in 1994, Kosovo in 1999, and Sudan more recently, generates interest in bolstering the capacity and will of the United States and its partners to respond.

Many of these studies and the lessons of experience teach that early preventative action is often critical to effective crisis response.[3] Deterring mass atrocities in the first place averts the human toll before it accumulates and is also sometimes easier than stopping atrocities once they start.[4] "Experience has constantly taught us," writes Gareth Evans, "that effective prevention is far less costly in blood and treasure than cure—than reacting only after many lives have been lost, a lust for revenge aroused, and reconciliation made that much harder."[5]

A recent task force on genocide prevention, chaired by Madeleine K. Albright and William S. Cohen, similarly emphasizes in its report the need for early, decisive action as mass atrocities loom or begin to unfold: "Even when signs of preparation for genocide are apparent, there are opportunities to alter leaders' decisions and interrupt their plans. By improving our crisis response system, we will be better prepared to mount coherent, carefully calibrated, and timely preventive diplomacy strategies."[6] This echoes a recommendation of a 2005 task force on the United Nations, chaired by Newt Gingrich and George Mitchell, that "the United Nations must create a rapid reaction capability among UN member-states that can identify and act on threats before they fully develop."[7] In January 2009 the UN secretary-general released his report on implementing the responsibility to protect, a normative concept discussed in the following section. One of three pillars of that strategy is "timely and decisive response," again recognizing that prompt and resolute action is critical to addressing crises of genocide and large-scale atrocities.

The 1999 crisis and NATO intervention in Kosovo generated particular public attention to the issues of humanitarian military intervention and questions about the adequacy of the UN-centered international legal system. By contrast, the more recent debate prompted by crises in Sudan and elsewhere has generally downplayed issues related to military intervention and international law regarding the use of force. There are several reasons for this relegation of military and legal issues.

One legacy of the 2003 Iraq invasion has been to suppress the political correctness of discussing armed intervention generally, and especially without strong UN Security Council backing. The very term *humanitarian intervention* is toxic to some audiences, and to the extent military intervention is discussed it is usually far down on the atrocity-prevention public and diplomatic agendas.

A further reason recent policy studies of atrocity prevention devote little attention to whether international legal rules regulating intervention are appropriate is that the issue is seen as a distant secondary consideration to political will.[8] "Summoning the political will to take risks is the main obstacle to converting the responsibility to protect into a program of action," concludes a prior Council Special Report upon which this report builds.[9] The task force on genocide prevention briefly discusses international norms when it recommends "promoting a system of international norms and institutions that averts potential genocide and mass atrocities before they occur, stops them quickly and effectively when they occur, helps societies rebuild in their wake, and holds perpetrators accountable."[10] But the bulk of its specific recommendations focus on the issues of political will, preventive diplomacy, and capacity-building.[11]

Notwithstanding the current reluctance in public discourse to emphasize military intervention and call into question international legal constraints on the use of force, the remainder of this report rests on three premises. First, coercive military measures to stop mass atrocities include a wide spectrum of activities, most far short of invasion and direct attacks on a regime's authority. Force or threat of force may be used in cases of genocide and mass atrocities to, among other things, protect vulnerable populations, guard relief efforts, degrade perpetrators' capacity for repression, and signal a willingness to escalate further if necessary. Military operations short of major invasion could include[12]

– securing/controlling transportation routes and borders;
– reinforcing peace operations;
– enforcing no-fly zones, safe havens, or arms embargoes;
– jamming broadcasts and other communications;
– precision-targeted strikes; or
– demonstrating presence.

Second, although military threats and force are rarely the primary tools for stopping mass atrocities, they remain important ones. Threats of military force can help deter systematic atrocities before they occur. Military measures can help stop ongoing atrocities by, for example, interposing forces between conflict factions or degrading a state's capabilities for repression. And intervention or the threat of it may be needed to back up other tools, such as international criminal law, diplomatic efforts, or economic sanctions.

Third, nonmilitary mechanisms are critical to stopping mass atrocities, and nonmilitary means are almost always a preferred option when effective. None of this is to deny that military intervention carries risks, including the possibility of spurring dangerous backlashes or causing its own direct human toll.[13] Nor is it to assert the primacy of military over nonmilitary means. Rather, this report takes as one of its premises the UN secretary-general's recent counsel that mass atrocity crises require "early and flexible response[s] tailored to the specific circumstances of each case," and that any sound strategy will combine many elements, most of them nonmilitary.[14]

International Norms of Intervention and Calls for Reform

Recognizing that timely and resolute international response is necessary to stop mass atrocities, and that in some cases the threat or use of military intervention may be one among many important elements of that response, events in Darfur raise again the question of whether the current international legal system is likely to facilitate the kind of early, decisive, and coherent action—especially with respect to military force—needed to effectively combat atrocity crimes.[15] That legal system, built primarily on the UN Charter, is designed (and for good reason) to prize deliberation and consensus-building over swift response, exhaustion of nonmilitary measures over rapid escalation. For most international crises, these features help keep the peace. But are they well suited for preventing mass atrocities?

INTERNATIONAL LAW AND INTERVENTION

It is widely held that as a matter of international law, the use of military force against or in another state is prohibited except in self-defense or when authorized by the UN Security Council. The UN Charter prohibits "the threat or use of force against the territorial integrity or political independence of any state,"[16] except in self-defense, and confers on the Security Council "primary responsibility for the maintenance of international peace and security."[17] In the event of threats to peace and security, the Security Council can take or authorize nonmilitary measures to restore them.[18] If the Security Council considers that nonmilitary measures would be inadequate or have proved inadequate, it may take such military action "as may be necessary to maintain or restore international peace and security."[19] In recent decades it has become generally accepted—especially after UN-authorized interventions in Haiti, Somalia, and Bosnia—that widespread atrocities occurring within states may pose threats to peace and security warranting Security Council action.[20]

There is currently no widely accepted right or license among individual states to humanitarian intervention, as there is one to self-defense.[21] The United States has generally interpreted its and other states' authority to use force more broadly than many of its allies, especially with regard to self-defense, but most states and legal experts agree that there is no clearly established international legal authority justifying armed intervention into another state to stop atrocities.[22] Although not universally held and subject to exceptions, especially in cases of genocide, this understanding of international law and of the UN Charter reflects a view that resorting to armed force is an evil to be avoided whenever possible.[23]

The idea of carving out an exception to the general prohibition on force in urgent cases of mass atrocities received a boost at the close of the twentieth century, with the international community's failure to intervene to stop genocide in Rwanda (1994) and NATO's intervention to stop Serbian ethnic cleansing in Kosovo (1999).[24] In the face of Serbian atrocities, the UN Security Council was deadlocked, with Russia and China threatening to veto any authorization of force. NATO intervened anyway, and a number of ex post facto statements from various states and state-sponsored commissions claimed that the intervention, though not strictly legal, was nevertheless legitimate.[25] If that were the case, some argued, why not articulate and establish a more general international norm of intervention to prevent similarly grievous harms? This would entail developing standards for permissible intervention, including requirements of necessity, proportionality, last resort, and the like.

A general doctrine of humanitarian intervention has not gained momentum since the Kosovo crisis, although the widespread view that intervention in the Kosovo case was appropriate at least calls into question the absolutist view that Security Council authorization is always required.[26] Russia and China remain hostile to it for both ideological and self-interested reasons.[27] Many states in the developing world and Southern Hemisphere oppose a right of humanitarian intervention, seeing it as eroding principles of sovereignty and as likely to be used as pretext for imperialism.[28] The United States and its European allies, too, have been reluctant to endorse such an approach as a general position, fearing it is prone to abuse.[29]

THE RESPONSIBILITY TO PROTECT

Although the idea of establishing an international legal doctrine of humanitarian intervention has generally foundered, the normative principle of the responsibility to protect has emerged in its place. A political rather than legal concept, the responsibility to protect focuses on a state's responsibilities toward its population and on the international community's responsibilities when a state fails to fulfill its own.[30]

At the 2005 UN World Summit, world leaders agreed by consensus in the final outcome document to the following points:

> Paragraph 138. Each individual State has the responsibility to protect its populations from genocide, war crimes, ethnic cleansing, and crimes against humanity. . . .

> Paragraph 139. The international community, through the United Nations, also has the responsibility to use appropriate diplomatic, humanitarian, and other peaceful means . . . to help protect populations from genocide, war crimes, ethnic cleansing, and crimes against humanity. In this context, *we are prepared to take collective action, in a timely and decisive manner, through the Security Council, in accordance with the charter, including Chapter VII, on a case-by-case basis and in cooperation with relevant regional organizations as appropriate, should peaceful means be inadequate and national authorities manifestly fail to protect their populations from genocide, war crimes, ethnic cleansing, and crimes against humanity* (emphasis added).

The responsibility to protect does not create any new legal obligations. But it is an important political tool for shaping the normative terrain of intervention in several respects. First, to those regimes that might perpetrate mass atrocities or allow them to occur within their borders, it rejects powerfully the argument that sovereignty shields them from international concern. Second, to the international community, it emphasizes a responsibility to act when a regime is in major breach of certain duties, thereby providing political momentum for action.[31]

The 2005 World Summit formulation, however, reflects a number of compromises, some problems of which are discussed below. Most significant, it reinforces the view that only the Security Council should administer collective action to enforce it. To many responsibility-to-protect proponents, this was seen as watering down the concept.[32]

Despite these compromise limitations, the responsibility to protect faces opposition or skepticism from a significant number of influential UN member states, including Russia, China, and many in the global south and those associated with the nonaligned movement. Some of this hostility is rooted in broader ideological debates over sovereignty and noninterference with internal matters, as well as with the uneven distribution of power in the Security Council. Some of it is due to perceptions that the United States and others intend to use the concept self-interestedly.[33] Some is also due to ambiguity of what exactly responsibility to protect means, in theory and in practice.

UN secretary-general Ban Ki-moon pledged to "operationalize" the responsibility to protect, and in January 2009 he published his proposed strategy for doing so.[34] That strategy emphasizes protection responsibilities of individual states, international assistance and capacity-building, and timely and decisive international response to crises. The secretary-general urged the UN General Assembly to act on this implementation plan, and in July 2009 that body held a debate that exposed significant international rifts. Many states, including the United States, pledged strong support for the responsibility to protect as others emphasized the importance of sovereignty and noninterference and some labeled it neocolonialist.[35]

CALLS FOR REFORM

Amid this context, the ongoing crisis in Darfur has reignited debate about whether armed intervention absent UN Security Council authorization is sometimes appropriate. In 2006, for instance, Susan Rice, now the U.S. permanent representative to the United Nations, along with Anthony Lake and Donald Payne, wrote: "The U.S. should press for a Chapter VII UN resolution that issues Sudan an ultimatum: accept unconditional deployment of the UN force within one week, or face military consequences. . . . If the U.S. fails to gain UN support, we should act without it as it did in 1999 in Kosovo."[36]

As discussed in greater detail below, an international legal regime that puts decisions about international intervention solely in the hands of the UN Security Council risks undermining the threat or use of intervention when it may be most potent in stopping mass atrocities. The features of the UN Charter that help resolve security crises peacefully make it difficult to generate the quick, decisive, and coherent action needed to deter or roll back mass atrocities. With several permanent Security Council members ideologically hostile to such interventions generally or self-interestedly hostile to specific interventions, rapid agreement or a credible escalatory threat is unlikely.[37]

Before a crisis, it is difficult for the international community to threaten sufficient costs to deter mass atrocities if potential perpetrators expect the UN Security Council to be unable to agree on a robust response. Once perpetrators begin to commit mass atrocities, deliberation by the UN Security Council often produces watered-down responses, because moving incrementally may be necessary to build broad enough support among its members and because deferring to even weak UN Security Council actions can serve as an excuse for member states not to take stronger action. And even if the Security Council eventually authorizes intervention, it is unlikely to do so quickly, because the requirements of broad consensus and the UN Charter's preference for exhausting nonmilitary means before considering military options has tended to produce incrementally escalating threats, sanctions, and other measures over long periods.

For those dissatisfied with a strict interpretation of the UN Charter, reform proposals tend to fall into four categories:

1. *Break the law when necessary.* This view holds that international law should generally continue to prohibit intervention absent UN Security Council authorization, but contemplates that in some exceptional circumstances, intervention without that authorization should be treated as morally and politically justified.[38] Some proponents of this view look to analogues in domestic criminal law, where criminal behavior is excused or punishment mitigated after the fact in light of exceptional circumstances of necessity.[39] Others look to Kosovo as an example, in which NATO intervention was widely viewed as legitimate, even if not strictly legal.[40] A variant of this view would rely on ex post facto validation of interventions by the UN Security Council when it is unable or unwilling to take adequate action in time to deal with a crisis. In the 1990s, for example, the UN Security Council approved intervention by Economic Community of West African States forces in Liberia and Sierra Leone only after

those forces had already gone in to forge and enforce ceasefires.[41] In any of these visions a major issue is the substantive criteria by which necessity should be judged, and proponents of this approach differ over whether these standards should be formulated and formalized in advance or articulated only as crises arise.

2. *Reform internal UN rules, standards, and procedures.* This view holds that the UN system is fundamentally sound but that it can be made more effective and efficient through soft law agreements between its members and through organizational reforms. A frequent recommendation is to urge the five permanent members to agree among themselves to not deploy their veto in humanitarian crises.[42] Others focus on the need for agreement among UN members on substantive standards to guide Security Council decision-making with regard to intervention.[43] Another way of streamlining UN Security Council decision-making is to build more standing UN early-warning and intervention capacity.[44] Common to proposals sharing this perspective is a confidence that the UN system can be made to perform better from within.

3. *Push for new legal doctrine of humanitarian intervention.* Those less confident in the UN Security Council's responsiveness urge development of a humanitarian intervention doctrine, similar to the way self-defense operates as an exception to the rule that only the UN Security Council can authorize coercive force.[45] As noted, this view gained some short-lived momentum following the 1999 Kosovo intervention. It never gained wide support, however, especially in light of concern that such a principle would be susceptible to abuse (states masking self-interested intervention as humanitarian), and of strong negative reactions from Russia, China, and countries of the nonaligned movement.[46]

4. *Create new international institutional bodies.* If exclusive reliance on the UN Security Council to authorize intervention fails to stop mass atrocities adequately, another alternative is to create new international institutions likely to be more responsive and effective. In recent years a common version of this approach proposes a standing coalition of democratic states that would act jointly when the Security Council does not.[47] Proponents believe that such intervention would be more legitimate than UN Security Council action (because it would be backed by commitment to liberal-democratic values)

and effective (because it would be less constrained by the need to satisfy at least all five permanent Security Council members). New international institutional arrangements could also build on existing ones, such as NATO, and would not replace the UN Security Council but instead stand ready to act when collectively deemed necessary among its membership.

Categories 1 and 2 are evolutionary reforms. They aim to preserve international law for the most part as it is, but improve its functioning. Categories 3 and 4 are radical reforms. Category 3 aims to change the substance of international law, whereas Category 4 aims to change the processes by which that law is applied.

These approaches are not mutually exclusive, but they do reflect different orientations toward the UN and different prioritization of policy interests and risks. As the following section explains, effective legal and policy reform requires striking the appropriate balance among these priorities.

International Norms and Effective Strategy

It is easy to say that policy failures like that of protecting Darfuris are not a problem of law, but of political will—where there is the will, the law is adequate (or will not stand in the way)—or of capabilities. But to dismiss a hard look at the law ignores the many ways in which international law shapes, amplifies, and organizes political will and capabilities. International law and norms with respect to the use of force play three major functions relevant to combating mass atrocities.[48]

First, they constrain military threats or intervention. Although international use-of-force rules "cannot divide the universe into mutually exclusive blacks and whites," they "help in differentiating the infinite shades of gray that are the grist of the decision-process" of states.[49] Even when law cannot prevent military action of dubious legality, it can make it more costly and therefore less likely or shape the way it is used or not used.

Second, they help legitimate appropriate preventive actions. Widely understood and respected rules can bolster or weaken political and diplomatic arguments for or against intervention. The persuasive power of legitimacy therefore links international law and norms to the political will all observers recognize as critical in addressing mass atrocities.

Third, they help coordinate the diplomacy through which preventive strategies are formulated and implemented. In establishing global or regional security forums, for example, law helps determine the processes through which states make joint decisions, and individual states plan for contingencies based in part on patterns of diplomacy and decision-making created or reinforced through law.

CONSTRAINTS ON TIMELY
AND DECISIVE ACTION

International legal rules and institutions for regulating armed force have never been able to eradicate aggression or allow intervention in all cases for which it is appropriate, but they affect the costs and risks states associate with military actions. A crucial policy question is therefore how international law and norms might adapt to better permit timely and decisive intervention or to help deter perpetrators without loosening too much existing constraints on aggression.

One problem alluded to earlier is that exclusive reliance on the UN Security Council to authorize intervention often erodes the credibility of threats to intervene, especially early in a crisis.[50] In the words of the task force on genocide prevention,

> In crafting preventive diplomatic strategies, care must be taken not to follow an overly rigid process or "escalatory ladder" with potential perpetrators. While a set of sequential steps is often necessary to gain international support and, moreover, demonstrate that peaceful alternatives have been exhausted to enhance the legitimacy of coercive ones, this approach can be exploited and "gamed" by adversaries to undermine the impact of diplomatic action. Stronger measures at earlier stages, though perhaps difficult to muster politically, often have a greater chance of success.[51]

The logic of deterrence is that by threatening enough action at the front end, the most forcible measures may not actually be needed.[52] But, in practice, the Security Council has tended to slowly escalate its collective response to mass atrocity crises only as each successive increment of pressure or intervention fails.[53] Exclusive reliance on the Security Council can therefore embolden perpetrators to present the international community with a fait accompli or to exploit rifts among members to stymie or water down collective responses. Even when military force is not ultimately used, the credible threat of it may be needed to strengthen nonmilitary efforts to deter or prevent further atrocities.[54]

The UN secretary-general's responsibility to protect implementation strategy aims to address this concern: "In a rapidly unfolding emergency situation, the United Nations, regional, subregional, and national decision makers must remain focused on saving lives through 'timely and decisive' action, not on following arbitrary, sequential or graduated policy ladders that prize procedure over substance and process over results."[55] But in the same paragraph it also emphasizes that "the more robust the response, the higher the standard for authorization."[56] In effect this creates a potential gap between what the Security Council (especially the five permanent members) can agree upon—especially in a timely manner—and what may be necessary to prevent or roll back ongoing atrocities.

From a U.S. policy perspective, the challenge is to move international law and norms in ways that strike a proper balance between permitting too much and permitting too little intervention. The United States is of course limited in its ability alone to shape international law, and one must also recognize that no balance point will ever be perfect and that where the balance is struck on issues of preventing mass atrocities may fortify or undermine the UN Security Council's authority on a range of other issues, including security threats. As it stands, however, in practice the strict interpretation of the UN Charter shared widely among other states and international bodies is often not agile enough to meet mass atrocity challenges.

LEGITIMATING INTERVENTION

A flip side of the constraining role of international law and norms, however, is their legitimating role: law and norms help justify intervention among domestic and international audiences and actors in ways that contribute to success in stopping mass atrocities.

One reason the perceived legitimacy derived from legal justification is critical to effectiveness is that it helps build and sustain political support for action. "Without question," concludes a recent study of intervention, "the presence of clear legal authority to intervene will also be highly significant in convincing other states that military action is legitimate.... Legality by itself is no guarantee of support, to be sure. But the absence of agreed legal authority can undermine the chances of building or sustaining a committed coalition."[57] The need to hold together international coalitions with legitimacy is important at the front end of intervention and also over time, because confronting mass atrocity crimes as well as their underlying causes often requires long-term commitment not only to coercive strategies but also to the political engagement and reconstruction efforts that must follow them.

A related way in which legitimacy ties to effectiveness of intervention is in building and sustaining partnerships with other international actors, including local regional organizations (such as the African Union or Organization of American States) and factions within a crisis country. If intervention leads to political transition, for example, the legitimacy of any new government is important to establishing peace and stability.[58] The effectiveness and credibility of transitional justice efforts to hold perpetrators accountable and promote reconciliation may depend on local and regional perceived legitimacy as well.[59]

Many of the features of the UN Security Council system cited as being heavily constraining are what generally infuse Security Council authorized actions with legitimacy. From a U.S. policy perspective, the challenge is to avoid steps to address the constraining effects of international law and norms in ways that erode the necessary legitimacy of actions.

COORDINATING STRATEGY AND OPERATIONS

The coordinating function of international law is important to effectiveness because military force or threats will be just one of many instruments brought to bear. Most strategies to deter or prevent atrocities will combine military, diplomatic, economic, and legal actions. Channeling decisions on the use of force through the UN Security Council, for example, has among its advantages bringing military actions within the same decision-making structure—and with the same crucial parties—as many decisions on the other instruments.

With respect to coordinating diplomatic responses to crises, the task force on genocide prevention emphasizes that consistency of message is critical to credible deterrents.[60] Consistent and organized international diplomacy helps prevent perpetrators from playing multiple negotiators off one another.

The coordinating role of law is also important because threats or deployments of military force will occur at the same time that other coercive tools are wielded. Consider the recent example of Sudan, in which UN Security Council efforts to ratchet up pressure while deploying peacekeepers have been made alongside unilateral financial sanctions by the United States as well as International Criminal Court (ICC) prosecutions of Sudanese leadership figures. The African Union—a regional body established through international law—is deploying the (albeit weak) peacekeeping force and has objected collectively to the ICC's prosecution of Sudanese president Omar al-Bashir. Although international law in this case does not produce consistency among the major policy instruments, it provides forums for diplomatic mediation and establishes some predictable rules for decision-making.[61]

The coordinating and legitimating roles of international law are critical not only to effective coercive diplomacy but also to managing the difficult tasks that follow. In that regard, the task force on genocide prevention also emphasizes the need to enlist regional partners—including neighboring states and local business communities and civic leaders—in crafting a long-term solution to underlying drivers of mass atrocities.[62] With respect to coordination on the ground, militaries need to work with a variety of different civil actors, "including national populations and local authorities, as well as international, national, and nongovernmental organizations and agencies."[63] International law, by organizing states and by endowing their joint decisions with politically authoritative weight, helps bring the various actors into the fold of international efforts to address crises.

Each of these coordinating functions of law—with respect to diplomatic messages, strategy and its instruments, and actors on the ground—is important to effective intervention in mass atrocity crises. Although the current international legal system often fails to align them well and is overly burdensome, efforts to operate outside established institutional structures must account for these coordination requirements before, during, and after coercive actions.

SUMMING UP

UN Security Council authorization is the mechanism by which intervention is most widely viewed as legitimate, and many states believe it is the only legal avenue. But the Security Council system is often slow or unwilling to take or threaten sufficiently robust actions to deal with mass atrocity crises. Overly restrictive legal rules or processes make it difficult to bring adequate pressure or force to bear. That said, the legit-imating and coordinating roles of international law are important to effectiveness in combating mass atrocities as well, and there will often be trade-offs among these functions: efforts to expand the latitude to use force often come at the expense of perceived legitimacy and abil-ity to coordinate efforts with other important international actors. The recommendations that follow therefore aim to reconcile the constrain-ing function of law with its legitimating and coordinating functions in combating mass atrocities.

Recommendations

Given the preceding analysis, this report recommends that the United States take steps to make the responsibility to protect a more powerful tool, and to position itself on the issue of whether the UN Security Council has a monopoly over applying forcefully that tool. To best combat the threat of mass atrocities consistent with other U.S. foreign policy interests and priorities, the United States should take independent steps and work with allies to improve the responsiveness of the existing UN Security Council and simultaneously prepare and signal a willingness, if the UN Security Council fails to act in future mass atrocity crises, to take necessary action to address them. This requires a careful diplomatic balance asserting strong support for a normative framework that facilitates timely and decisive intervention but not provoking backlash among states already hostile to existing or emerging norms that limit sovereignty.

At least in the short run, radical reform options—such as pushing immediately for an international legal doctrine of humanitarian intervention or developing new international institutions to deliberate collectively on military intervention—are unlikely to effectively reconcile the requirements of flexibility of action with legitimacy and coordination. Neither is likely to gain widespread support at this time among states in the global south and among the nonaligned movement, let alone from China and Russia. A doctrine of humanitarian intervention aims to trade legitimacy of the process by which the UN Security Council authorizes force for legitimacy based on purpose, and proposals for new international groupings such as a coalition of democracies aims to trade it for legitimacy based on participating states' values. A problem for both of these radical options is that too many critical states will opt out, undermining both legitimacy and coordination of resulting action in the eyes of many audiences.

Given that other instruments, such as sanctions and international criminal justice, will often be administered through and legitimated by UN Security Council action, the United States has a strong interest in effective Security Council functioning. The intervention issue with respect to mass atrocities cannot be completely divorced from issues of the Security Council's status more generally; steps that erode its authority in one area are likely to erode it in others, in ways detrimental to U.S. interests.

That said, the possibility that the United States and its allies might move toward radical reform is useful in pressing others for evolutionary improvements to existing law, by raising the specter that failure to generate enough UN Security Council responsiveness could undermine its own legitimacy and embolden calls for radical alternatives. If the system built on UN Security Council primacy continues to fray because only by acting outside it can states address moral and political emergencies of vast proportion, then defenders of that system must work to make it operate better.[64] Furthermore, radical reform options—such as advancing a legal doctrine of humanitarian intervention or proposing alternative institutional arrangements to the UN Security Council— stand a better chance of gaining adherents down the road as necessary if the United States is seen as having credibly led and assisted efforts to improve the existing framework.

The United States should express strong support for the responsibility to protect—but that support must be carefully nuanced and timed.

The Obama administration has already taken several important steps to promote the concept, including a June 2009 address on the issue by Ambassador Rice in Vienna.[65] It should follow up these communications with an administration-wide policy statement, perhaps using the forthcoming presidential National Security Strategy document, to be followed by the Pentagon's National Defense Strategy, committing to further implementing the responsibility to protect. Such a statement should emphasize the nonmilitary aspects of the responsibility to protect, including preventive diplomacy and cultivating effective, local rule-of-law institutions—but also express strong commitment of military resources and readiness to intervene when necessary.

The timing and framing of strong U.S. commitments to the responsibility to protect are critical, because the United States cannot be seen as owning the concept if it is to succeed. The UN General Assembly debate in July 2009 on the responsibility to protect highlighted substantial skepticism among many states, especially China and nonaligned movement states, and some states are intent on branding it as a U.S. or colonialist tool. U.S. statements must therefore be integrated with other elements of an overall diplomatic strategy that walks the fine line between pushing too aggressively and too feebly.

In supporting the responsibility to protect, the United States should emphasize appropriate limits on Security Council vetoes.

Commonly discussed recommendations that the permanent five members of the UN Security Council jointly forswear the use of their veto authorities in cases of urgent humanitarian need are unrealistic any time soon. China and Russia are especially unlikely to disarm themselves of the veto power. The United States, too, should be wary of ceding its veto power given the propensity of other blocs of states to invoke the responsibility to protect in unduly politicized ways.

Yet the veto issue is important because the mere possibility of its use by one or more permanent members can slow Security Council decision-making, water down its collective response, and embolden perpetrators of atrocities. Although joint agreement among the permanent five powers with respect to their veto authority is improbable, the United States can take valuable independent steps in the way it discusses its Security Council role and veto authority in articulating its policy.

In affirming its own commitment to the responsibility to protect, the United States should declare that each of the five permanent Security Council members has a special responsibility to uphold global norms and that the veto power should not be used to block timely and decisive action when genocide or crimes against humanity are manifestly occurring and when other criteria, such as necessity and proportionality of military action, are satisfied. Framing the issue this way does not impair the United States' ability to protect its interest in the Security Council, but articulating conditions under which the veto should not be used—especially if reinforced by other similarly minded permanent members—would help raise the political costs of threatening to veto strong resolutions in urgent circumstances. Acknowledging special responsibilities that come with permanent Security Council status—including not only responsibilities to act in crises but to support capacity-building efforts and other preventive measures—would also help foster backing for the responsibility to protect among states of the developing world and nonaligned movement, which view skeptically the concept and U.S. efforts to promote it.

The United States should encourage like-minded allies to issue similar or joint political statements on atrocity prevention and Security Council vetoes, while redoubling diplomacy on these issues with the Southern Hemisphere.

In the short term, similar statements from allies like Britain and France would reinforce the U.S. message supporting the responsibility to protect and the deterrent value of pledging in advance strong crisis response. Down the road, these discussions and the resulting statements could form the basis, if necessary, for new international legal doctrine—while in the meantime they could facilitate decision-making upon commonly agreed and understood criteria.

At least as important as coordination with like-minded allies in the Northern Hemisphere is diplomatic engagement with the Southern. The United States has much work to do to convince wary audiences— especially in Africa, Latin America, and Southeast Asia—that the responsibility to protect is not a general license for interference in other states' internal affairs, that it aims to address only the most egregious systematic violations of universal norms, and that it does not emphasize military over nonmilitary solutions. In Africa, for example, the discussion of the responsibility to protect should be paired with commitment to building and working with AU conflict prevention and peacekeeping capabilities. And in each of these regions are influential states more receptive to the responsibility to protect with which the United States should try to work in crafting a joint approach.[66] Whereas the United States should seek united public positions on these issues with its European partners, political sensitivities demand that much of the diplomacy with the Southern Hemisphere be conducted more quietly, to avoid public splits or diplomatic efforts by others to spoil productive dialogue.

There may be temptations to apply the responsibility to protect concept broadly as a means of mobilizing political support for action in a wide range of crises. For example, in 2008, France's foreign minister invoked the concept to mobilize international action on Myanmar's inadequate care for cyclone victims. However imperfect the 2005 World Summit statement may be, its restricted application to four types of crisis—those involving genocide, war crimes, crimes against humanity, and ethnic cleansing—carries the imprimatur of universal state assent. Although the United States and its partners should stand ready to act in that broader array of contingencies, emphasizing depth over breadth of the responsibility to protect ensures better chance of wide support among critical states.[67]

The United States should emphasize the responsibility to protect and the need for timely and decisive action in its diplomacy on other multilateral legal issues.

The United States should integrate discussion of atrocity prevention and the responsibility to protect with its diplomacy on both UN Security Council reform and the International Criminal Court, to advance its positive vision of international norms as well as to avoid outcomes that further complicate the challenges of deterring and stopping mass atrocities.

A concern with UN Security Council reform is that expansion of the current membership structure would likely weaken the ability of the Security Council to respond in a timely and decisive way to mass atrocity crises. Shifting geopolitical balances since the UN Charter's founding have undermined the Security Council's legitimacy, as the membership distribution—and especially the veto-wielding and permanent status of the five main World War II victorious powers—reflects less and less contemporary global power distribution. Increasing the size of the Security Council—as all major reform proposals would do—would, however, likely slow its decision-making rather than streamline it. Moreover, some of those states with the strongest claims to a greater Security Council role under the most plausible reform proposals—India, for example—tend to be ideologically skeptical, if not hostile, to humanitarian intervention and what they view as threats to state sovereignty.

While avoiding direct linkage between the two issues, the United States should use its bilateral dialogues on Security Council reform to press its message about the need for improved international responses to mass atrocities and make clear that it regards as unacceptable any reform proposal that undermines rather than improves the Security Council's effectiveness in addressing such crises. This diplomacy will likely be more effective if paired with a strong policy statement such as the one described regarding veto power.

A concern with the ICC is that the likely addition of *aggression* to crimes over which the prosecutor and court have jurisdiction could further complicate international responses to mass atrocity crises. At the 2010 Conference of States Parties, member states will consider adding the crime of aggression to the court's purview (under the original treaty establishing the ICC, this issue was deferred until the review conference). Depending on that conference outcome, intervening without clear UN Security Council authorization could open participating states' leaders to ICC charges. Even if prosecution seems far-fetched, additional legal uncertainty and liability will at least slow decision-making with regard to mass atrocity crises absent swift Security Council authorization.

The United States should participate as a nonparty observer in remaining preparatory discussions on the crime of aggression issue, and the implications for the responsibility to protect and responding to mass atrocity crises should feature heavily in U.S. government deliberations about its participation in the 2010 conference. It should make sure that due consideration is given to how a crime of aggression provision could affect the international community's capacity and willingness to address mass atrocity crises. It should further make clear to its allies and other state proponents of the ICC that the outcome of the crime of aggression issue could undermine any momentum behind the United States' cautious but growing engagement with the ICC.

The United States should prepare to operate in cases of urgent necessity absent UN Security Council authorization.

The strategy laid out in this report emphasizes improving the Security Council's functioning through unilateral and multilateral efforts that help raise the costs of actions that slow or thwart its responsiveness. That said, the United States should be prepared to act outside the Security Council if necessary. Although it should not go so far as to declare in advance an explicit intention to do so, the United States should not completely hide its willingness to do so either.

For policymakers, this means being prepared to act within a legal gray zone when the moral calculus so dictates. Military and civilian contingency planners should actively consider scenarios for which Security Council action is neither present nor immediately forthcoming.[68]

Operating in an international legal gray zone will require tremendous investments of political and diplomatic capital, especially with respect to allies reluctant to act without clear legal authority. But the potential payoff can be high not only in terms of immediate humanitarian imperatives but also in shaping the future legal environment in ways more responsive to such needs. As the Kosovo crisis shows, operating this way in cases of urgent humanitarian necessity inevitably shapes the future normative terrain, especially as international bodies react ex post facto and the precedential value of actions are debated. For the United States, this means it must conduct its diplomacy and justify publicly its actions in ways to promote long-term a more protective regime. Meanwhile, those states skeptical of or hostile to a more human rights–protective regime must come to see it as in their own long-term interests to facilitate rather than undermine timely and decisive action.

Endnotes

1. It also builds on earlier Council on Foreign Relations work, including its 2007 report *Darfur and Beyond*, which emphasized operational capacity issues. Lee Feinstein, *Darfur and Beyond: What is Needed to Prevent Mass Atrocities,* Council Special Report No. 22 (New York: Council on Foreign Relations Press, 2007).

2. *Norms,* in this sense, represents a broader category of behavior expectations than law, insofar as not all norms are legally obligatory. Peter J. Katzenstein, "Introduction," in Peter J. Katzenstein, ed., *The Culture of National Security: Norms and Identity in World Politics* (New York: Columbia University Press, 1996), p. 5.

3. Richard Haass, *Intervention: The Use of American Military Force in the Post-Cold War World* (Washington, DC: Brookings Institution Press, 1999), pp. 88–90.

4. Barry Posen, "Military Responses to Refugee Disasters," *International Security*, vol. 21, no.1 (summer 1996), pp. 72–111.

5. Gareth Evans, *The Responsibility to Protect: Ending Mass Atrocity Crimes Once and For All* (Washington, DC: Brookings Institution Press, 2008), p. 79.

6. Madeleine K. Albright and William S. Cohen, *Preventing Genocide: A Blueprint for U.S. Policymakers,* a genocide prevention task force report (United States Holocaust Memorial Museum, The American Academy of Diplomacy, and the Endowment of the United States Institute of Peace, 2008) p. xxiii.

7. Newt Gingrich and George Mitchell, *American Interests and UN Reform: Report of the Congressional Task Force on the United Nations* (Washington, DC: United States Institute of Peace, 2005), p. 28.

8. Gareth Evans argues that mobilizing political will among domestic audiences, national political leaders, and the international community is crucial to ensuring that the international community fulfills its responsibility to protect. Evans, *The Responsibility to Protect,* pp. 223–41.

9. Feinstein, *Darfur and Beyond*, p. 46.

10. Madeleine Albright and William S. Cohen, *Preventing Genocide,* p. xxiii.

11. Ibid, pp. xvi–xviii.

12. Ibid, pp. 82–83; and Posen, "Military Responses to Refugee Disasters," pp. 78–79.

13. For an excellent analysis of the conditions for effective humanitarian intervention, see Taylor B. Seybolt, *Humanitarian Military Intervention: The Conditions for Success and Failure* (New York: Oxford University Press, 2007). For skeptical views on the effectiveness of humanitarian military intervention, see, for example, Alan J. Kuperman, *The Limits of Humanitarian Intervention: Genocide in Rwanda* (Washington, DC: Brookings Institution Press, 2001); and Conor Foley, *The Thin Blue Line: How Humanitarianism Went to War* (London: Verso, 2008).

14. Ban Ki-moon, *Implementing the Responsibility to Protect: Report of the Secretary-General* (United Nations document A/63/677, January 12, 2009), p. 2.

15. *A More Secure World: Our Shared Responsibility,* a report of the UN High-Level Panel on Threats, Challenges and Change (United Nations, 2004), at paragraph 42: "We have been struck once again by the glacial speed at which our institutions have responded to massive human rights violations in Darfur, Sudan."

16. *Charter of the United Nations,* chapter 1, article 2.

17. Ibid, chapter 5, article 23.

18. Ibid, chapter 7, articles 39–41.

19. Ibid, article 42. United Nations General Assembly (UNGA) resolution 377 A, known as the Uniting for Peace resolution, states that, in cases where the UN Security Council fails to act in order to maintain international peace and security because of disagreement between its five permanent members, the matter shall be addressed by the general assembly. However, given that the UNGA has no authority under the UN Charter to authorize military action, the legality of any intervention based on this resolution is questionable at best.

20. Evans, *The Responsibility to Protect,* p. 134. The UN Charter also encourages regional arrangements—consistent with the UN's purposes and principles—to take enforcement actions if necessary, but again the charter stipulates that Security Council authorization is required. *Charter of the United Nations,* chapter 8.

21. Evans, *The Responsibility to Protect,* p. 137; Thomas M. Franck, *Recourse to Force: State Action Against Threats and Armed Attacks* (Cambridge: Cambridge University Press, 2002) pp. 135–73; and Bruno Simma, "NATO, the UN and the Use of Force: Legal Aspects," *European Journal of International Law,* vol. 10, no.1 (March 1999).

22. Abraham D. Sofaer, "International Law and Kosovo," *Stanford Journal of International Law,* vol. 36 (2000), p. 1; D. Stephen Mathias, "The United States and the Security Council," in Niels Blokker and Nico Schrijver, eds., *The Security Council and the Use of Force: Theory and Reality—A Need for Change?* (Netherlands: Brill Academic Publishers, 2005), pp. 181–82. According to Sean Murphy, "there exists considerable confusion and disagreement about the contemporary parameters of the *jus ad bellum*; if you were to ask a random group of legal advisers to foreign ministries their views on whether, for example, humanitarian intervention, or using force to rescue nationals abroad, or a cross-border raid against a terrorist camp, are permissible under the *jus ad bellum,* you are likely to receive varied answers: some saying yes; some saying no; some insisting that it depends on the circumstances; and some refusing to respond to the question." Sean D. Murphy, "Protean Jus Ad Bellum," *Berkeley Journal of International Law,* vol. 27 (2009), p. 23.

23. In the words of Italian international jurist Antonio Cassese, "Under the UN Charter system . . . respect for human rights and self-determination of peoples, however important and crucial it may be, is never allowed to put peace in jeopardy. One may like or dislike this state of affairs, but so *it is under lex lata* [or law as it exists]." Antonio Cassese, "Ex iniuria ius oritur: Are We Moving towards International Legitimation of Forcible Humanitarian Countermeasures in the World Community?" *European Journal of International Law,* vol. 10 (1999), p. 25. The Genocide Convention, however, states that "Contracting Parties confirm that genocide, whether committed in time of peace or in time of war, is a crime under international law which they undertake to prevent and to punish," which arguably creates an affirmative obligation to intervene when necessary. *Convention on the Prevention and Punishment of the Crime of Genocide,* (United Nations document E/447, June 26, 1947), article I.

24. With regard to Rwanda, the main problem was lack of political will to intervene.

25. For an example of one such commission, see *The Responsibility to Protect: Report of the International Commission on Intervention and State Sovereignty,* ICISS (December 2001).

26. W. Michael Reisman, "NATO's Kosovo Intervention: Kosovo's Antinomies," *American Journal of International Law*, vol. 93 (1999), p. 860.

27. Vladimir Baranovsky, "Humanitarian Intervention: Russian Perspectives," and Chu Shulong, "China, Asia and Issues of Intervention and Sovereignty," in *Pugwash Occasional Papers: Intervention, Sovereignty and International Security*, vol. 2, no. 1 (2001), http://www.pugwash.org/publication/op/opv2n1.htm.

28. Ralph Zacklin, "Beyond Kosovo: The United Nations and Humanitarian Intervention," *Virginia Journal of International Law*, vol. 42 (2001), pp. 935–36.

29. During and immediately after the Kosovo crisis, the United Kingdom and Belgium came closest to asserting a legal right to humanitarian intervention in that case. They both pulled back, however, from staking out a general position on humanitarian intervention, and other major European states were quick to deny that the Kosovo intervention established legal precedent in favor of humanitarian intervention because of its unique facts. Jane Stromseth, "Rethinking Humanitarian Intervention: The Case for Incremental Change," in J. L. Holzgrefe and Robert O. Keohane, eds., *Humanitarian Intervention: Ethical, Legal, and Political Dilemmas* (Cambridge: Cambridge University Press, 2003), pp. 234–37; Adam Roberts, "NATO's 'Humanitarian War' Over Kosovo," *Survival*, vol. 41 (September 1999), pp. 102–23.

30. Francis M. Deng, *Sovereignty as Responsibility: Conflict Management in Africa* (Washington, DC: Brookings Institution Press, 1996).

31. The UN Security Council reaffirmed paragraphs 138 and 139 of the World Summit Outcome Document (United Nations document A/60/L.1, September 15, 2005) in Resolution 1674 (United Nations document S/RES/1674, April 28, 2006). Note, however, that paragraph 139 appears to emphasize an affirmative responsibility to act only with respect to nonmilitary means.

32. Edward C. Luck, *The United Nations and the Responsibility to Protect*, Stanley Foundation Policy Analysis Brief, August 2008, p. 3.

33. According to former UN undersecretary general for political affairs Sir Kieran Prendergast, "In 1999, the secretary-general made his single most significant speech, which was on the right of humanitarian intervention. The nonaligned hate the concept, and nonaligned foreign ministers and the G77 at the summit level rejected the existence of any concept of a right of humanitarian intervention with a few months. You don't have to be a genius to work out that the responsibility to protect is just turning the [humanitarian intervention] coin over, but it doesn't actually change the coin." "Reform and Progress in the United Nations: Interview with Sir Kieran Prendergast," *Fletcher Forum of World Affairs*, vol. 30 (winter 2006), http://fletcher.tufts.edu/forum/archives/pdfs/30-1pdfs/prendergast.pdf

34. Ban Ki-moon, *Implementing the Responsibility to Protect.*

35. "Responsibility to protect: An idea whose time has come—and gone?" *The Economist*, July 23, 2009. The UN General Assembly ultimately adopted a weak resolution agreeing to hold further discussions on the issue.

36. Susan E. Rice, Anthony Lake, and Donald Payne, "We Saved Europeans. Why Not Africans?" *Washington Post*, October 2, 2006.

37. As Daniel Byman and this author observed in 2002, "In almost any conceivable [humanitarian] intervention, the United States and its allies will have far more capabilities than the local opponents do, but they will often lack the will and capability to use force effectively. Highly motivated adversaries are likely to exploit any limits, perhaps enabling them if not to triumph, then at least to deny the United States and its allies full or quick success." Daniel Byman and Matthew Waxman, *The Dynamics of Coercion: American Foreign Policy and the Limits of Military Might* (Cambridge: Cambridge University Press, 2002), p. 200.

38. *Humanitarian Intervention: Legal and Political Aspects*, Danish Institute of International Affairs (1999), pp. 77–95.

39. Michael Byers and Simon Chesterman, "Changing the Rules About Rules?" in J. L. Holzgrefe and Robert O. Keohane, eds., *Humanitarian Intervention: Ethical, Legal, and Political Dilemmas* (Cambridge: Cambridge University Press, 2003), pp. 198, 203.

40. ICISS report.

41. Franck, *Recourse to Force*, pp. 155–62.

42. Those proposing such an agreement include, among many others cited in this report: Franck, *Recourse to Force*, pp. 155–62; Feinstein, *Darfur and Beyond*, pp. 22–23; and the genocide prevention task force report.

43. Kofi A. Annan, *In Larger Freedom: Towards Development, Security and Human Rights for All* (United Nations document A/59/2005, March 21, 2005), p. 33.

44. Feinstein, *Darfur and Beyond*, pp. 22–23. The Gingrich-Mitchell report argues that the lack of centralized control of peacekeeping forces, because of individual state micromanagement, is a problem that needs to be addressed by strengthening the oversight given by the UN's Department of Peacekeeping Operations (ibid, p. 11).

45. *Kosovo Report*, a report of the Independent International Commission on Kosovo (Oxford: Oxford University Press, 2000), pp. 187–98. Some have suggested that humanitarian intervention could be justified legally as a form of collective self-defense. For example, see George P. Fletcher and Jens David Ohlin, *Defending Humanity: When Force Is Justified and Why* (Oxford: Oxford University Press, 2008).

46. *Final Document* of the Non-Aligned Movement XIII Ministerial Conference, Cartagena, Colombia, April 8–9, 2000, paragraph 263 (http://www.nam.gov.za/xiiimin-conf/final4.htm): "We reject the so-called 'right' of humanitarian intervention, which has no legal basis in the UN Charter or in the general principles of international law."

47. Ivo Daalder and James Lindsay, "Democracies of the World, Unite," *American Interest* (January/February 2007); Ivo Daalder and Robert Kagan, "The Next Intervention: Legitimacy Matters," *Washington Post*, August 6, 2007, http://www.washingtonpost.com/wp-dyn/content/article/2007/08/05/AR2007080510156.html; G. John Ikenberry and Anne-Marie Slaughter, *Forging a World of Liberty under Law: U.S. National Security in the 21st Century*, final report of the Princeton Project on National Security, Woodrow Wilson School of Public and International Affairs, Princeton University, 2006; John McCain, "League of Democracies" speech delivered to the Hoover Institution, May 1, 2007, http://www.cfr.org/publication/13252/.

48. This framework is adapted from that laid out by former State Department legal adviser Abram Chayes in his work *The Cuban Missile Crisis* (New York: Oxford University Press, 1974), in which he writes of "law as constraint," "law as justification," and "law as organization."

49. Ibid, pp. 102–03.

50. As Micah Zenko writes, "Intervening early can be far more effective in terms of combat casualties and the number of troops involved than larger, much more costly interventions later in the crisis. Responding rapidly to credible reports of mass violence will avoid being presented with a *fait accompli* on the ground to confront opponent forces before they can seize key territory and commit more murders. Arriving to a combat theater later limits the interveners' options to manage the conflict in a way that is beneficial to their forces and tactics." Micah Zenko, "Saving Lives with Speed: Using Rapidly Deployable Forces for Genocide Prevention," *Defense and Security Analysis*, vol. 20 (2004), p. 3.

51. Genocide prevention task force report, p. 69.

52. Posen, "Military Responses to Refugee Disasters," pp. 84–86. Posen asserts that "if the Bosnian Serbs had genuinely believed they faced the force that defeated Iraq, then they

would likely have behaved rather differently than they did early in the Bosnian war" (ibid. p. 85).

53. British foreign secretary Jack Straw raised these concerns with respect to Sudan in 2004. Ewen MacAskill, "Straw Urges UN Reform and Attacks Response to Darfur," *Guardian,* September 3, 2004.

54. As now-ambassador Rice noted in 2007 congressional testimony, effective political and diplomatic action in situations like Darfur must be "married with the credible threat of powerful sanctions and the use of force." Susan E. Rice, "Dithering on Darfur: U.S. Inaction in the Face of Genocide," testimony before the Senate Foreign Relations Committee, delivered April 11, 2007, http://foreign.senate.gov/testimony/2007/Rice-Testimony070411.pdf. "U.S. military assets," concludes the genocide prevention task force report, "can also play an important role in supporting and providing credibility to options short of the use of force," p. xxiii.

55. *Implementing the Responsibility to Protect, a report of the Secretary-General,* paragraph 50, pp. 22–23.

56. Ibid.

57. Jane Stromseth, David Wippman, and Rosa Brooks, *Can Might Make Rights? Building the Rule of Law after Military Interventions* (New York: Cambridge University Press, 2006), pp. 18–19.

58. William J. Durch, with Tobias C. Berkman, "Restoring and Maintaining Peace," in William J. Durch ed., *Twenty-First-Century Peace Operations* (Washington, DC: United States Institute of Peace and the Henry L. Stimson Center, 2006), pp. 1, 18.

59. Laura A. Dickinson, "The Promise of Hybrid Courts," *The American Journal of International Law*, vol. 97, no. 2 (April 2003), pp. 295–310.

60. Genocide prevention task force report, p. 71.

61. For example, the UN Security Council, which referred the Sudan situation to the ICC as part of its slow escalation of pressure, also has authority to defer for periods of time the resulting prosecutions.

62. Supra note 63. The Gingrich-Mitchell report of the Task Force on the United Nations also emphasizes the importance of involving regional actors in preventing genocide, p.16. For a discussion of the organizational capacity of different institutions, see Victoria K. Holt, *The Responsibility to Protect: Considering the Operational Capacity for Civilian Protection*, a discussion paper of the Henry L. Stimson Center, January 2005, http://www.stimson.org/fopo/pdf/Stimson_CivPro_pre-pubdraftFeb04.pdf.

63. Evans, *The Responsibility to Protect*, p. 222.

64. As Michael W. Doyle argues, "The mere fact that unilateral action could be considered legitimate should have a responsibility-inducing effect on the Security Council. Rather than enjoying a monopoly, the council will now know that its actions are subject to the 'market' of alternative judgment." *Striking First: Preemption and Prevention in International Conflict* (Princeton: Princeton University Press, 2008), p. 62. Mary Ellen O'Connell argues to the contrary, that only by rejecting arguments for bypassing the Security Council will it be possible to improve its functioning. "The United Nations Security Council and the Authorization of Force: Renewing the Council Through Law Reform," in Niels Blokker and Nico Schrijver, eds., *The Security Council and the Use of Force: Theory and Reality—A Need for Change?* (Netherlands: Brill Academic Publishers, 2005), p. 47.

65. Remarks by Ambassador Susan E. Rice, U.S. permanent representative to the United Nations, on the UN Security Council and the responsibility to protect, at the International Peace Institute Vienna Seminar, June 15, 2009.

66. Notably, article 4 of the Constitutive Act of the African Union prohibits the use of force against and interference in the internal affairs of other member states, but it also

declares "the right of the Union to intervene in a Member State pursuant to a decision of the Assembly in respect of grave circumstances, namely war crimes, genocide
and crimes against humanity." See http://www.africa-union.org/root/au/AboutAu/
Constitutive_Act_en.htm.

67. As David Scheffer argues, "A broader mandate for R2P in the years ahead may burden
it with so much political controversy and dissent among international lawyers that it
will collapse as a declared commitment, even with respect to atrocity crimes, before
it has an opportunity to be tested." "Atrocity Crimes Framing the Responsibility to
Protect," *Case Western Reserve Journal of International Law*, vol. 40 (2007–2008), p.
115. The United States has an interest in establishing forceful but narrow interpreta-
tions of the responsibility to protect also because some of the triggers mentioned in
the World Summit outcome statement are susceptible to politicized interpretation.
Genocide and *crimes against humanity* are relatively well-defined terms in international law and imply a very high threshold of action and intention by perpetrators.
Ethnic cleansing is less well defined, and *war crimes* is subject to wide interpretation.
Although the drafters probably intended the latter term in this context to refer only
to widespread and systematic atrocities, its inclusion could be used to justify outside
intervention in any number of internal or international conflicts. The broader point
is that in working to shape international law and norms to better serve its policy imperatives, the United States must worry also about moves by other states that could
derail or dilute U.S. efforts.

68. For more on what this would look like, see genocide prevention task force report,
chapter 5.

About the Author

Matthew C. Waxman is adjunct senior fellow for law and foreign policy at the Council on Foreign Relations. He is also associate professor at Columbia Law School and a member of the Hoover Institution task force on national security and law. Mr. Waxman previously served at the U.S. Department of State, as principal deputy director of policy planning. His prior government appointments included deputy assistant secretary of defense for detainee affairs, director for contingency planning and international justice at the National Security Council, and special assistant to the national security adviser. He is a graduate of Yale College and Yale Law School, and studied international relations as a Fulbright scholar in the United Kingdom. After law school, he served as law clerk to Supreme Court justice David H. Souter and U.S. Court of Appeals judge Joel M. Flaum. His previous publications include *The Dynamics of Coercion: American Foreign Policy and the Limits of Military Might* (with Daniel Byman, Cambridge University Press, 2002).

Advisory Committee for
Intervention to Stop Genocide and Mass Atrocities

Elliott Abrams, *ex officio*
Council on Foreign Relations

Gary J. Bass
Princeton University

John B. Bellinger
Arnold & Porter LLP

Sunil B. Desai
U.S. Marine Corps

James F. Dobbins
RAND Corporation

David F. Gordon
Eurasia Group

John Hillen
Global Defense Technology & Systems, Inc.

Victoria K. Holt
Henry L. Stimson Center

Nancy A. Jarvis
Farrand Cooper, P.C.

Larry D. Johnson
Columbia University School of Law

Neil Kritz
U.S. Institute of Peace

Edward C. Luck
International Peace Institute

Scott Malcomson
New York Times Magazine

John A. Nagl
Center for a New American Security

Suzanne A. Nossel
Human Rights Watch

Victoria Nuland
National Defense University

Raymond C. Offenheiser
Oxfam America

Stewart M. Patrick, *ex officio*
Council on Foreign Relations

W. Michael Reisman
Yale Law School

David B. Rivkin
Baker & Hostetler LLP

David J. Scheffer
Northwestern University School of Law

Kristen L. Silverberg

Paul B. Stares, *ex officio*
Council on Foreign Relations

Jane E. Stromseth
Georgetown University Law Center

Daniel C. Twining
The German Marshall Fund of the United States

Ruth Wedgwood
Paul H. Nitze School of Advanced International Studies, Johns Hopkins University

Clint Williamson
U.S. Department of State

William D. Zabel
Schulte, Roth & Zabel

James D. Zirin
Sidley Austin LLP

Mission Statement of the International Institutions and Global Governance Program

The International Institutions and Global Governance (IIGG) program at CFR aims to identify the institutional requirements for effective multilateral cooperation in the twenty-first century. The program is motivated by recognition that the architecture of global governance—largely reflecting the world as it existed in 1945—has not kept pace with fundamental changes in the international system. These shifts include the spread of transnational challenges, the rise of new powers, and the mounting influence of nonstate actors. Existing multilateral arrangements thus provide an inadequate foundation for addressing many of today's most pressing threats and opportunities and for advancing U.S. national and broader global interests.

Given these trends, U.S. policymakers and other interested actors require rigorous, independent analysis of current structures of multilateral cooperation, and of the promises and pitfalls of alternative institutional arrangements. The IIGG program meets these needs by analyzing the strengths and weaknesses of existing multilateral institutions and proposing reforms tailored to new international circumstances.

The IIGG program fulfills its mandate by

- Engaging CFR fellows in research on improving existing and building new frameworks to address specific global challenges—including climate change, the proliferation of weapons of mass destruction, transnational terrorism, and global health—and disseminating the research through books, articles, Council Special Reports, and other outlets;

- Bringing together influential foreign policymakers, scholars, and CFR members to debate the merits of international regimes and frameworks at meetings in New York, Washington, DC, and other select cities;

– Hosting roundtable series whose objectives are to inform the foreign policy community of today's international governance challenges and breed inventive solutions to strengthen the world's multilateral bodies; and

– Providing a state-of-the-art Web presence as a resource to the wider foreign policy community on issues related to the future of global governance.

Council Special Reports

Published by the Council on Foreign Relations

Sovereign Wealth and Sovereign Power: The Strategic Consequences of American Indebtedness
Brad W. Setser; CSR No. 37, September 2008
A Maurice R. Greenberg Center for Geoeconomic Studies Report

Securing Pakistan's Tribal Belt
Daniel Markey; CSR No. 36, July 2008 (Web-only release) and August 2008
A Center for Preventive Action Report

Avoiding Transfers to Torture
Ashley S. Deeks; CSR No. 35, June 2008

Global FDI Policy: Correcting a Protectionist Drift
David M. Marchick and Matthew J. Slaughter; CSR No. 34, June 2008
A Maurice R. Greenberg Center for Geoeconomic Studies Report

Dealing with Damascus: Seeking a Greater Return on U.S.-Syria Relations
Mona Yacoubian and Scott Lasensky; CSR No. 33, June 2008
A Center for Preventive Action Report

Climate Change and National Security: An Agenda for Action
Joshua W. Busby; CSR No. 32, November 2007
A Maurice R. Greenberg Center for Geoeconomic Studies Report

Planning for Post-Mugabe Zimbabwe
Michelle D. Gavin; CSR No. 31, October 2007
A Center for Preventive Action Report

The Case for Wage Insurance
Robert J. LaLonde; CSR No. 30, September 2007
A Maurice R. Greenberg Center for Geoeconomic Studies Report

Reform of the International Monetary Fund
Peter B. Kenen; CSR No. 29, May 2007
A Maurice R. Greenberg Center for Geoeconomic Studies Report

Nuclear Energy: Balancing Benefits and Risks
Charles D. Ferguson; CSR No. 28, April 2007

Nigeria: Elections and Continuing Challenges
Robert I. Rotberg; CSR No. 27, April 2007
A Center for Preventive Action Report

The Economic Logic of Illegal Immigration
Gordon H. Hanson; CSR No. 26, April 2007
A Maurice R. Greenberg Center for Geoeconomic Studies Report

The United States and the WTO Dispute Settlement System
Robert Z. Lawrence; CSR No. 25, March 2007
A Maurice R. Greenberg Center for Geoeconomic Studies Report

Bolivia on the Brink
Eduardo A. Gamarra; CSR No. 24, February 2007
A Center for Preventive Action Report

After the Surge: The Case for U.S. Military Disengagement from Iraq
Steven N. Simon; CSR No. 23, February 2007

Darfur and Beyond: What Is Needed to Prevent Mass Atrocities
Lee Feinstein; CSR No. 22, January 2007

Avoiding Conflict in the Horn of Africa: U.S. Policy Toward Ethiopia and Eritrea
Terrence Lyons; CSR No. 21, December 2006
A Center for Preventive Action Report

Living with Hugo: U.S. Policy Toward Hugo Chávez's Venezuela
Richard Lapper; CSR No. 20, November 2006
A Center for Preventive Action Report

Reforming U.S. Patent Policy: Getting the Incentives Right
Keith E. Maskus; CSR No. 19, November 2006
A Maurice R. Greenberg Center for Geoeconomic Studies Report

Foreign Investment and National Security: Getting the Balance Right
Alan P. Larson and David M. Marchick; CSR No. 18, July 2006
A Maurice R. Greenberg Center for Geoeconomic Studies Report

Challenges for a Postelection Mexico: Issues for U.S. Policy
Pamela K. Starr; CSR No. 17, June 2006 (Web-only release) and November 2006

U.S.-India Nuclear Cooperation: A Strategy for Moving Forward
Michael A. Levi and Charles D. Ferguson; CSR No. 16, June 2006

Generating Momentum for a New Era in U.S.-Turkey Relations
Steven A. Cook and Elizabeth Sherwood-Randall; CSR No. 15, June 2006

Peace in Papua: Widening a Window of Opportunity
Blair A. King; CSR No. 14, March 2006
A Center for Preventive Action Report

Neglected Defense: Mobilizing the Private Sector to Support Homeland Security
Stephen E. Flynn and Daniel B. Prieto; CSR No. 13, March 2006

Afghanistan's Uncertain Transition From Turmoil to Normalcy
Barnett R. Rubin; CSR No. 12, March 2006
A Center for Preventive Action Report

Preventing Catastrophic Nuclear Terrorism
Charles D. Ferguson; CSR No. 11, March 2006

Getting Serious About the Twin Deficits
Menzie D. Chinn; CSR No. 10, September 2005
A Maurice R. Greenberg Center for Geoeconomic Studies Report

Both Sides of the Aisle: A Call for Bipartisan Foreign Policy
Nancy E. Roman; CSR No. 9, September 2005

Forgotten Intervention? What the United States Needs to Do in the Western Balkans
Amelia Branczik and William L. Nash; CSR No. 8, June 2005
A Center for Preventive Action Report

A New Beginning: Strategies for a More Fruitful Dialogue with the Muslim World
Craig Charney and Nicole Yakatan; CSR No. 7, May 2005

Power-Sharing in Iraq
David L. Phillips; CSR No. 6, April 2005
A Center for Preventive Action Report

Giving Meaning to "Never Again": Seeking an Effective Response to the Crisis in Darfur and Beyond
Cheryl O. Igiri and Princeton N. Lyman; CSR No. 5, September 2004

Freedom, Prosperity, and Security: The G8 Partnership with Africa: Sea Island 2004 and Beyond
J. Brian Atwood, Robert S. Browne, and Princeton N. Lyman; CSR No. 4, May 2004

Addressing the HIV/AIDS Pandemic: A U.S. Global AIDS Strategy for the Long Term
Daniel M. Fox and Princeton N. Lyman; CSR No. 3, May 2004
Cosponsored with the Milbank Memorial Fund

Challenges for a Post-Election Philippines
Catharin E. Dalpino; CSR No. 2, May 2004
A Center for Preventive Action Report

Stability, Security, and Sovereignty in the Republic of Georgia
David L. Phillips; CSR No. 1, January 2004
A Center for Preventive Action Report

To purchase a printed copy, call the Brookings Institution Press: 800.537.5487.
Note: Council Special Reports are available for download from CFR's website, www.cfr.org.
For more information, email publications@cfr.org.